"Instead of
Antidepressants"

# THE
# LAUGH

Interactive book #1A

by GL

**DORRANCE PUBLISHING CO., INC.**
PITTSBURGH, PENNSYLVANIA 15222

ISBN # 0-8059-6897-0

Printed in the United States of America

*First Printing*


For information or to order additional books, please write:
Dorrance Publishing Co., Inc.
701 Smithfield Street
Third Floor
Pittsburgh, Pennsylvania 15222
U.S.A.
1-800-788-7654
Or visit our web site and on-line catalog at
www.dorrancepublishing.com

# FOREWORD
# AND
# DISCLAIMER

The purpose of this issue is to make you laugh! A team of researchers from Nothingdamn University has conducted a remarkable test on a group of 96 people (48 men and 48 women). A daily dosage of antidepressants using by these people was replaced by a reading of our previous issue of "The Laugh. An interactive book #1". The result was stunning! All 96 (100%!) decided to abolish antidepressants for good and have subscribed to all future issues of "The Laugh". Even 52 shrinks who prescribed these antidepressants and were using them more frequently than their patients, decided to quit! You can read the results in the next issue of "New Richmond Journal of Medicine". That is why we call this issue an "Interactive book 1A" (not book #1) and we changed our motto in the upper right corner of cover sheet from "Stuff ready to laugh" to "Instead of antidepressants".

There are plenty of misspelled words and incorrect grammar constructions inside- they are made on purpose to prompt an active participation on your part in the process of interacting.

You are welcome to make all necessary corrections and answer all the questions in all the quizzes. We suggest also a reading of this issue as a supplement to a reading of your favored magazine with a colorful picture of a cover girl with only the vicinity around the vagina, the anal opening and the breast nipples being covered and all the other body parts, required for the penis erection and a fruitful masturbation, being uncovered.

All names and titles are fictitious. Except for a former Soviet Union, all the actions and events take place in an imaginary country- Divided Regions of Antarctica.

Any similarities with real people and entities are unintentional and can not become a basis for any court actions. The readers and particularly warned against comparing the life and the people in the Divided Regions of Antarctica with the life and the people in the United States of America.

# GLOSSARY

1. Brandon, Lolita
   Wife of a former Secondary State Treasurer Michael Brandon. After a naïve gal Nancy Cougar have performed an Historic oral sex sessions on a penis of a former Secondary State Treasurer, Lolita Brandon in unison with the husband was playing a fool rejecting allegations of an affair as an assault on an integrity of former Secondary State Treasurer's penis. Later, utilizing the scandalous "procratch-do not procratch" game, Lolita ran for a seat in a Secondary Tier and won it. After this she received millions for a book about the lovely time she and Nancy have by sharing the penis of a former Secondary State Treasurer. Now Lolita is preparing for a run (together with Nancy) for a Prime Administrator position.

2. Brandon, Michael
   Former Secondary State Treasurer of the Divided Regions of Antarctica, a charming stud with a playful penis. Adventures of his penis led to a tragic events after his Administration term was expired. While the whole country including the Cute Information Authority and the Fine Bureau of Information was busy analyzing the romantic relationship between his penis and the mouth of naïve gal Nancy Cougar, the enemies have plenty of time to prepare their hits.

3. Divided Regions of Antarctica (DRA)
   An imaginary country.

4. Jury
   A sophisticated weapon utilized by the lawyers and the judges to conduct their criminal activity by screwing up ours, the antarctidians, brains. Similar to a murder weapon used by the murderers.

   Part of a shameless bloody show performed by the lawyers and the judge called a "trial".

12 non-professionals who must decided who's performance is better. As shown by recent DNA testing, jury sent innocent people to prison for long period of time and let go free the murderers, rapists, swindlers e.t.c.

The tool used by the lawyers/judges to continue to utilize the antiquated justice system to keep and multiply their profits at the expense of human lives.

By the utilization of the brains of only 12 (why 12? Why not 12 millions?) jurors, the lawyers/judges create an illusion that the **PEOPLE** of the DRA are making the final decision. That's how the lawyers/judges making fools from the antarctidians. That's how we are screwing up ourselves!

5. Lawyer
   Person practicing the law (refer to definition of "Practicing the law" below)

6. Lie
   An universal tool for screwing up the people's brains in order to achieve certain goals. In the Divided Regions of Antarctica mostly used by the politicians, bureverends, priests with violent penises, lawyers/judges and playboys.

7. Oral Sex
   The importance of oral sex sessions in a political career of former Secondary State Treasurer M. Brandon is described in meticulous details in a new book by M. Brandon in Chapter Four: **"Blow job and it's role in making monetary and foreign policy decisions"**.

8. Penis
   A male organ of generation. The influence of the penis on political and cultural life in the Divided Regions of Antarctica thoroughly described in a new book of former Secondary State Treasurer M. Brandon in Chapter One: **"My penis-my life!"**, in Chapter Two: **"How my penis survived the procratchment scare"** and in Chapter Three: "How I and my wife became millionaires by capitalizing on the adventures of my working **hard** penis".

   The latest developments in science and technology (namely the development of Hujagra) made it possible for the penis to achieve the strengths powerful enough to have sex with multiple vaginas in short period of time (refer to vagina definition below). A classic example is the penis of a rich and famous owner of a respectable half porno magazine "Goodboy". The said penis is enjoying it's golden age by having intercourse with a dozen different vaginas every day, while the females –the vagina holders- are seeking the chance to show their vaginas and surrounding areas for public review in the above referenced magazine in order to become rich and famous.

9.  Playboy
    A male with an adventurous penis (refer to a penis definition above) that navigates multiple vaginas (refer to a vagina definition below) resulting in a dramatic influence on the course of History. There are several types of playboys in the Divided Regions of Antarctica. The most famous are playboys- Prime Administrators, playboys- Secondary State Treasurers, playboys- bureverends and playboys- priests.

10. P.M.L!
    Pardon My Language!

11. Practicing the law
    Process of raping the law by the lawyers and the judges.

12. Prime Administrator
    President of an imaginary country- Divided Regions of Antarctica.

13. Procratchment
    A political game performed by the lawyers and the judges in order to multiply their profits. While the whole DRA country including the Fine Bureau of Information and the Cute Information Authority was kept busy with the analysis of the procratchment process, the country was left vulnerable. It took a long time to measure the weight of the sperm from the Secondary State Treasurer Michael Brandon's testicles on Nancy's dress to figure out that the weight of the sperm is not sufficient for the procratchment.

14. Secondary Tier
    The highest floor in the Building of the Government in the Divided Regions of Antarctica.

15. TANIYANA
    The Association of New Immigrants- You And New Antarctidians. This organization helped new immigrants from former Soviet Union to settle in Old Croy City.

16. UFO
    Unidentified flying object. In front of everybody in the Divided Regions of Antarctica, the lawyers have proved to the jury that the UFO crew members killed several people in the Divided Regions of Antarctica (during the famous trial of a murderer that was acquitted by the jury, although the scientific evidence clearly identified who did the murders). A brilliant example of a criminal work performed by good lawyers. After this process lawyers become rich and famous, a movie and TV stars, and enjoying the good life spending the money covered in the blood of the victims.

17. Vagina

The canal leading from the female external organ of generation to the unknown and enigmatic place .Used by the penis for the navigation back and forth and from left to right (refer to penis definition above). Mutual relationship between vagina and penis during the course of the History of human life led to a political, financial and military cataclysms, although was not completely and thoroughly analyzed by the scholars.

Vagina still remains the most convenient place for penis accommodation during the intercourse, despite a strong competition from the mouth, the fist and the anal opening, which took a large percentage of the functions performed before solely by vagina.

Like all others commodities in DRA, the vagina can be sold and resold repeatedly many, many times, although the law in DRA prohibits the sale of vagina at discount rates. The female –the vagina holder-in this case is labeled as "a prostitute" and can get a jail time for doing so. On the contrary, if the vagina is sold for thousand or millions of dollars, the female –the vagina holder-become not only rich but become very respectable in the DRA society. The classic examples are some famous Pollipood Actresses and some top models. But a real champion was and still is the famous wife of a performer Secondary State Treasurer James Filip Kramer who sold the vagina for billions of dollars to a billionaire Bypussys from Nemetia (another fictitious country). Contrary to the car sale, the value of vagina is increasing after each use. The value of a brand new vagina (a virgin) is practically close to zero.

18. WASA

**W**onderful **A**mbitious **S**ociety of **A**stronauts.

19. We

Residents of an imaginary country- the Divided Regions of Antarctica. "We" also equals to "Antarctidians".

20. YRS

**Y**our **R**evenue **S**ubtraction.

# ADVENTURE
# IN
# LITERATURE

About the emigration from a real country- former Soviet Union- into an imaginary country-the Divided States of Antarctica.

Once upon a time there was a lovely family of four symbols: Haim- an ingenious inventor , his short but heavy wife Surka (with 350 lbs of weight before bowel movement and 300 lbs after bowel movement) his sister Dwosiya (with practically no curves but tall) and Dwosiya's husband- a "goy" Wasiya –a heavy drinker with a huge child producing organ.

All four together with another family-a single mother with a daughter-a student in a medical school- have occupied apartment in Building #14 on Merzkaiya Street in a famous Ukrainian city on Black Sea-Odessa. One room which comprised at the same time a bedroom, a living room, a study, a library, a dining room, a conference room, a parlor, a sunroom, a recreation room, a storage room and a guest room, was completely their's and they share with the other family a kitchen, a toilet, a shower and a den.

Their room was very small and when Wasiya was sexually excited there was no space for his penis expansion and the ingenious inventor Haim was forced to provide an opening in the wall between their room and a common den (which they call a "sex hole") and Dwosiya was enjoying a "doggie style"(P.M.L!) sex with the outside part of Wasiya's penis in a den to a joyful excitement of a young neighbor-a student in a medical school.

By observing these intercourse sessions she not only had enhanced her own masturbation technic by synchronizing both movements-Dwosiya's on a Wasiya's prick and her own fingers, but also received high grades at the mid-term exams surprising the professor in medical school by describing the intercourse in such vivid details that even the experienced professor himself never heard about.

The first Surka's orgasm during the sex in missionary's position was explosive in direct sense and was remembered by almost half of the world. Due to unusually short length of Haim's penis and unusually big Surka's belly, the sex in the missionary position was consisting only of a squeezing the Surka's belly (which made Surka very horny and eventually led to her orgasm) and gentle touching by Haim's penis about the vagina's vicinity. After repetitive squeezing of Surka's stomach during the first night intercourse (after wedding ceremony) the gas pressure inside the stomach had build up to a critical point and the first Surka's orgasm was accompanied with a powerful and an audible anal emission of intestinal gases. The energy of the exhausted gases was equal to the energy released by a mid-size earthquake and all seismological stations positioned in Europe had registered enigmatic earthquake which puzzles the seismologists around the globe since the epicenter of an earthquake was positioned in the area never before experienced the earthquakes. Fortunately, the direction of the main thrust of the gas emission was due to Black Sea so there were no human lives perished, although the hide tides in the oceans were registered as far from Odessa as Japan.

During his leisure time Haim was practicing yoga, exercised in figure skating, jogging and weight lifting. For jogging and weight lifting Haim decided to utilize unusual curves and tremendous weight of Surka's body. While jogging could be performed by Haim himself, the weight lifting required another person, and Haim invited his friend Moishe for dividing the total weight of the Surka's body between them. Both voluntarily undertook a course of a young soldier in Soviet Army, training the legs and arms for weight lifting. After successful completion of the course and even receiving a special diploma, they were ready for Surka.

Several enema sessions were performed on Surka's stomach together with an application of a special multi-purpose press invented by Haim for the fat extraction from the Surka's body. At the end of the procedures Haim and Moishe were able to cut the Surka's weight to approximately 240 lbs down from the original 350 lbs(before bowel movement) allowing Moishe and Haim to enjoy the weight lifting.

Every morning Surka and Dwosiya have filled up beautifully crafted crystal tumblers with an accumulated during the full night sleep fresh urine and, after pronouncing loudly the toast to a robust health, have drunk the above referenced urine. These procedures (so called "urotropija") were performed in a strict accordance with a scientific breakthrough by the Russian medical researchers claiming that this urine recycling heels all the illnesses known to the humans. The only drawbacks of the procedures were the smell emanating from the mouths and the elevated levels of the urine in Surka's and Dwosiya's brain cells.

All four symbols were cheerfully employed. Haim was a mechanic on a plant that manufactured metal cans during the day time and the mines for the Army during the night time. Surka was an employee in a cafeteria in the same plant. Dwosiya work in the kindergarten and Wasiya was a fireman.

In addition to spying on each other, everybody in a former Soviet Union was stealing the items that were connected with their employment, whether it was a razor blade or a light bulb. The amount of pilfered goods was in straight proportion with a position held by a thief-the higher the position the heavier was the loot.

Surka and Dwosiya were, of course, no exceptions to this rule. Dwosiya was stealing the meat and the cheese intended to be consumed by the kindergarten's children replacing the stolen items with a fairy-tales about the meat and the cheese and showing the children the colorful pictures of said items. The kindergarten's manager was stealing the same meat and the same cheese in the amount approximately three times higher than the Dwosiya's amount plus she was also stealing all stock of the oranges and half of the stock of the milk.

Since Surka was working in a cafeteria, in a close proximity to the food, the volume and the weight of stolen goods were much higher. Besides, the ingenious inventor Haim found a brilliant way to cover the operation. The main dishes in the cafeteria were a "Borscht", a famous Russian food, and the cutlets. Once a month, there was a government inspection to check the fat content in the "Borscht". In accordance with the Russian health laws the more fat is in the food, the healthier is the food. Haim then decided to utilize this laws to their own advantage. He invented a multi-purpose press for the fat extraction from Surka's body, and at the day before the inspection Surka was lifted above the giant caldron where the "Borscht" was prepared, the press was applied to the Surka's body causing the fat pouring out of Surka's pores into the caldron raising the fat content in the "Borscht". This was enough to pass the inspection. The inspectors have measured the fat content, received the allocated bribe and have signed the paper certifying that the cafeteria had satisfactory passed the inspection. As a prize, additional fat pieces of meat and the sausage were given to Surka and Haim by the cafeteria manager.

Due to Surka's guts unique texture, the large quantities of consumed fat food produced the gases with tremendous energy. Surka was exhausting these gases constantly, and Haim was completely bewildered with the ideas of building a huge reservoir for the gas collection and a construction of a pipe line connecting Odessa with a capital of former Soviet Union-city of Moscow, to utilize the gas energy in several possible options. One of his idea-the utilization of these gases for rocket fuel for the earliest developments of Russian spacecraft- "Sputnik"-was met with a serious consideration by Russian Academy of Science and only the bureaucracy and remote location of Odessa from Moscow did not allow this to happen. The idea to use the gas energy for the heating and cooking in a new developed part of Russian capital was about to materialize but the emigration of four symbols had killed the event.

Wasiya was a fireman. Since there were no private insurance companies in former Soviet Union, the fires were so rare that in 14 years of Wasiya's experience as a fireman, the fire occurred only once. Wasiya was so excited that his penis become hard; Wasiya's colleagues used his tool as a fire hose, and a small fire was quickly extinguished by virtue of Wasiya urinating upon it.

By the end of the eighties the life in former Soviet Union become very hard. The jews have eaten all the food in the country and have drunk up almost of the potable water, so the Russian government decided to let the jews to emigrate. Even a "goy" Wasiya was allowed to leave the country. They sold almost all their belongings and for the money received they bought a diamond in order to smuggle it. The major obstacle, of course, was the famous Custom in Belorussian city of Brest. But the ingenious inventor Haim had a good plan.

Just before passing the custom gates, he had swallowed the diamond together with a full glass of specially developed liquid substance to create minor constipation in the stomach in order to hold the guts contents for a least 36 hours. When the custom officers saw Haim and Dwosiya, there were no doubts in their mind that these symbols are not carrying anything illegal. So Haim and Dwosiya have passed the custom without any problems. When "the goy" Wasiya came to the checkpoint, the only actions performed by the custom officers was a joint lifting of Wasiya's penis by two officers to exercise the arm muscles and to check the space between the penis and testicles for possible concealment of a bottle or two of very famous and very expensive Russian vodka "Stolichnaiya" with the ubiquitous nameplate "Made in USSR".

Once the custom officers saw Surka, the situation become completely different. Surka's body layout was an ideal storage for the variety of goods and classified information material that were prohibited to leave the country. Besides, the data, received from an informant-the conductor of the train's wagon, carrying our symbols- suggested, that something fishy is going on inside Surka's vagina. Two custom officers (#11 and #17) have lifted Surka's body in the air, turned her upside down and have spread her legs apart. Two other custom officers (#13 and #15) were summoned for the emergency operation. Custom officer #13 had inserted a huge shovel inside Surka's private area, swung several items the shovel from the left side to the right side and then from the top to the bottom through the thick layers of fat, while #15 with a flush light helped him with the navigation, lighting the way. They were hoping to find a highly classified scientific notes regarding Russian nuclear arsenal inside the Surka's vagina. But all they found were several pieces of indigestible sausages in plastic envelopes. The plastic envelopes were confiscated since the famous words "Made in USSR" were imprinted on them.

Finally, on July 11 at 1.20 p. m European time our four characters say "good-bye" to Soviet Union and after 24 hours by train have arrived in Vienna, Austria.

Now imagine a men's toilet in the right wing on 2$^{nd}$ floor of the hotel "Zum Turken" in Vienna. At 2 p.m local time the hotel in question was overwhelmed by a heavy stinky smell coming from the above referenced toilet. It was Haim producing the diamond into a special pot. After successfully given birth to the diamond, Haim carefully hide it in a private place since there were a lot of swindlers around the emigrants. They sell and buy everything: from cameras to jewelry, from toilet paper to watches. With this diamond in three months our four symbols have arrived in Old Kroy –the largest city in the Divided Regions of Antarctica.

## 1.  HAIM & SURKA

Soon after our four symbols have settled in Prooklyn, Old Kroy, the scientists all over the world have registered sharp ozone depletion in Prighton Peach area of Prooklyn where our characters have rented an apartment. On emergency session in Montreal, Canada it was a major topic of discussion and it was decided to track exactly the source and the full scope of unusual phenomena. Precise sensors were employed to track the source to Prighton $6^{th}$ street and pinpoint the gases coming out of back orifice of Surka but in two days Haim signed a contract with WASA (Refer to Glossary for WASA deciphering) to utilize the Surka's gas energy for astronaut's training.

Special load of sausages from the State of Old Ersey (made with a special additives to enhance Surka's gas production ability) was flown by a chopper to a Russian food store on Prighton Peach Avenue for consumption by Surka. A tight plug specially developed by Haim was inserted into Surka's rectum in order to collect and to contain gases inside the Surka's body. In approximately 6 days the gases inside were at the energy level required by WASA's specifications. Surka was flown by a special charter plane accompanied with two Rentagon fighters F-17 to Puston, Tixas-WASA's training facilities.

Surka was positioned on her stomach, a platform with two astronauts –on her buttocks. A 2.34 ton load was lifted by a special crane, the ropes holding the load were cut and the load by free fall with tremendous speed hit the Surka's back squeezing the stomach and initiating the gas exhaust. The plug was thrown out of Surka's rectum and was found later 3.9 miles from the Surka's body in a large hole after damaging a control tower of a local airport. The platform with two astronauts reached a point 320 miles above the planet Earth and the astronauts were enjoying this space journey. The only drawback of the experiment was a small aftershock by residual gases inside the Surka's stomach which produced several tornadoes in the neighboring states. But ingenious inventor Haim utilized even the aftershock for a source of energy for an operation of several wind mills to produce the electricity in the amount necessary to light up several villages in the Southern portion of the State of Tixas. Although the contract with WASA suppose to be for a long period of time, the government's money vault soon become empty after the government has to pay the lawyers researching all aspects of a romantic encounter between the former Secondary State Treasurer Michael Brandon's penis and the mouth of a naïve girl Nancy Cougar and a hundreds of lawyers successfully winning the frivolous lawsuits in courts against the major cities in the Divided Regions of Antarctica. The government was on the brink of bankruptcy, so the solution was to cut the money for the scientific programs. The contract between Haim and WASA was terminated, and Haim was pushed to find new ways for making the living. After meticulous analysis of the different approaches to the ways to become rich and famous, Haim found

7

the light at the end of the tunnel. He organized a band to explore vast possibilities in the show business. Two leading guitarists, a drummer, Haim, Surka, and Dwosiya become in a couple of months a very popular band under the name "Butterflies". The band become a foundation of a new direction in Pop Music, namely a "Gas Rap Music". The layout of the band on the stage was as follows.

The center and the left side of the stage was occupied by Surka dressed in a pink tricot. The enormous hills on the Surka's body were carefully underlined by the red and purple accessories. The multipurpose press custom modified by Haim was encircled around the Surka's belly. Inside the press separate solenoids controlled by Haim were stringing the different parts of the belly with sharp plungers exerting the pressure upon the belly and initiating the gas exhaust. By feeding Surka with a special food, the gases start producing the sound. The frequency and the magnitude of the sound was correlated with the belly spot under the pressure and the type of food consumed. This was achieved after Haim contacted leading gastroenterologists and famous physicists. After gases exited the anal orifice, they travel thru the maze of sound filters and a tank with a special chemical solution (to eliminate the odor). At the end of the gas travel itinerary another tank with another chemical solution (the formula being developed by Haim) for gas coloring in a coordination with the sound was located together with several microphones. Microprocessor control of the solenoids by the computer allowed Surka to produce the full spectrum of sound frequencies.

The right side of the stage was occupied by two leading guitarists, Dwosiya and the drummer. Haim was positioned in the rear background and was a conductor of the band. As soon as the first gas bubbles from Surka's belly start producing the first round of the sounds for a particular song, Dwosiya (after removing tight pants from the leading guitarists) start performing an oral sex on both guitarists alternatively. The guitarists start shouting into the microphones from the joy of the oral sex while the drummer used the drumsticks for spanking Dwosiya's buttocks coated with special sound producing laquer, initiating specific sounds into a microphone hanging above the buttocks and supported from the ceiling. After the guitarists have unloaded their boiling loads during the orgasm into the screaming crowd, they were so exhausted that they have to crawl to the backstage and recuperate themselves by using cocaine and heroin. Dwosiya instead continued to perform the sex act with a huge custom made microphone and her part was culminated after she also had an orgasm with a microphone inside her vagina. The brilliantly orchestrated band performance had initialized mass masturbation among the fans. By the end of the performance, not only men have painful orgasms but also 80% of women were unloading themselves 'fountainwise". The other 20% of the women trying to catch the sperm of the guitarists with their hands and mouths to use the sperm later for a skin massaging, as a souvenirs and to make a special cocktails for an immediate consumption. The men that were strong enough and still have the sperm available for unloading for a nominal fee were accommodated by Dwosiya after the show. The auditorium floor was flooding with the embryo producing components. Ingenious inventor Haim made a contract with the auditorium owners not to clean the place planning to conduct a special cloning experiments but Prime Administrator and Secondary Tier of the Divided Regions of Antarctica by a special decree have prohibited the cloning, and all the places where the band was performed were cleaned, after the federal moneys were received by the States (after declaring the places of performance as an emergency disaster areas). Haim was nominated for a Nobel Prize in chemistry for the invention of the solution for coloring Surka's gases and for the coating on Dwosiya's buttocks. After 17 performances Surka suddenly became ill and lost almost completely the gas producing ability. The doctors recommended not to consume light fat free food but the return to previously consumed heavy and fatty food. After the old diet was reinstated, Haim was unable to tame the explosive nature of the gases. Besides, on the South had emerged a new powerful Gas Rap band and the leader of this band in secret conversation with Haim promised to make a little rearrangements of the parts of Haim's body, namely to exchanged the places of Haim's head and Haim's penis. Haim was forced to dismantle the band. But by that time the 250,000 recorded copies were sold all over the world returning big bucks for the members of the band. Haim decided to use the part of his share to buy highly advertised by one of the tabloids a special equipment and materials for the penis enlargement. The manufacturers promised the penis enlargement of not less than 2 inches. But when 2 inches was finally achieved, Haim with an awe discovered that the penis had changed in it's shape and the look of the penis become similar to a question mark look. After the consultation with his lawyer Haim decided to sue the tabloid and the penis enlargement machinery's manufacturer for several million dollars. The case is still pending in courts.

Although in Haim's, Surka's and Dwosiya's Soviet Union's passports was written in the Nationality column word "Jew", practically it was a stinking joke of the Russian Government. The faith in God in Russia was replaced by faith in Communist Party and the Government, there were no synagogues, no Yiddish or Hebrew languages (only Russian), no Jewish culture at all. Haim was practically a man without any knowledge of any religion. It was very easy for him to open a brand new business.

He and two partners created a religious sect under the name "Combined Way to God". In the book written by the partners the three foundation stones for a new religion were described: 1. The Christian philosophy; 2. Consumption of a kosher food; 3. The ability for the man to have up to 18 wives provided he can satisfy them financially and the strength of his penis was sufficient to satisfy them sexually. (By the way, this was a main objective of the creation of the new sect-to provide each penis of each sect founder with the multiple vaginas!). The main business operation of the new sect was to attract millions of people who were interested to invest their money into purchase of a condominiums in the other world, closing day being the same day the person passed away. They also promised to spend part of the money invested to buy the forgiveness for all the sins that the person committed.

After month long campaign on TV and radio advertisements, money start pouring in from the people all over the world. Even Prime Administrator of the Divided Regions of Antarctica bought what was described in the offering plan released by the partners as a Penthouse in one of the condominiums with a magnificent ocean view and a God's Headquarters on the horizon. Even for the homeless people the construction of modern type shelters with the air conditioning was promised, prompting thousands of homeless people to send money to buy the room in the shelter instead of using the money for the drugs and the booze. The money received by the partners were used primarily for each partner, each partner's 18 wives and 18 lovers, personal needs such as vacations, shopping sprees, condominiums in this world, etc. Of course, the competition was not sleeping. After a year the YRS received hundreds of letters and telephone calls claiming the fraud by the partners. But the partners have a good lawyers who had promptly replied that the construction of the condominiums is in full swing and invited the YRS inspectors to visit the construction site. After unsuccessful contacts with WASA to check the site by utilization of a very powerful Hubbell telescope and even with the UFO crew to visit the site, the YRS decided to kill couple of their officers and send them to the other world for the site inspection.. The case is now under Supreme Court consideration.

During one of the routine complete physical examination, Surka suddenly was diagnosed with a rare form of diabetes-a saturation of exhaust gases with sugar. Haim immediately recalled his experiments with Surka's exhaust gases in former Soviet Union and in two month, after creation of a special solidifier and aftercooler,he was able to produce a granulated sugar in quantities enough to sign a contract with DRA Government to deliver tons of sugar for an export and trade on a world market. The Government successfully won the trade war against a neighbor-a socialistic state of Cluba and it's dictator Pisdrel Fastov. Haim invested the money received from the Government into a new joint venture with two prominent chemists. The main task of the venture was the conversation of all three wasted substances from Surka's body in order to fight an oil crisis as follows:

1.  Vaporous substance (gases)-into a hydrogen-for the development of a new energy source for automotive engines:
2.  Solid substance (regular waste from the anal opening)-into a crude oil;
3.  Liquid substance (urine)-into a pure gasoline.

After the first months the brilliant experiments result in a cost reduction of gasoline in average 8 cents per gallon on all gas stations throughout DRA and a jump in Doe Jones Industrial index 16 points in average.

After one month of producing hydrogen, crude oil and pure gasoline, Surka's skin become yellow, the octane number of gasoline fell below standard, and fighting oil crisis by Surka was stopped. The doctors recommend the use of low-carbs Batkins diet in order to heal the skin. In three month of utilization of Batkins diet, Surka's body layout was drastically changed. The belly was pushed to a rear end of Surka's body, leaving in front almost flat surface. Haim was very satisfied with these changes, since the rear end space was sufficient for jogging by both friends-Haim and Moische, who had recently emigrated from Russia and had occupied an apartment in a building two blocks away.

2. WASIYA.

The existence of a clean and not so expensive alcoholic beverages led to a tragic events. Realizing his ability of fulfilling the antarctidian dreams, Wasiya had commenced heavy drinking and on December 15, at 2.57 p.m. Eastern time (11.57 a.m Pacific time) Wasiya had suddenly passed away. Three remaining symbols were in a shock not because they loved him very much and missed him but because of the necessity of funeral expenses. But ingenious inventor Haim found a solution. He invited an underground rabbi Mr. Fukas who also emigrated from Odessa. Mr. Fukas performed a circumcision on a dead Wasiya's penis for a reasonable fee. Then the representative from Taniyana-the organization that helped new immigrants in Old Kroy City-was invited. The representative from Taniyana had observed the circumcised penis and had certified Wasiya as a jew. After this the Taniyana had paid all funeral expenses.

After a week Wasiya become a ghost and now in fool moon nights he rapes the women at the north-east corner of $8^{th}$ Avenue and $42^{nd}$ Street near Prot Authority Bus Terminal.

3. DWOSIYA

The most dramatic transformation had occur with a skinny and very tall Dwosiya whose bone structure layout represented an ideal background for plastic surgery experiments developed in the Divided Regions of Antarctica to a very elevated level of perfection (the rumor is that even a brain replacement was recently performed on a young actress by a cab driver, who even didn't have a doctor's license!). During the first plastic surgery, Dwosiya's breasts were increased 6 times, the buttocks were increased 2 times, the size of vagina was decreased 12 times, the wrinkles were removed from the Dwosiya's face and the inner surface of the vagina's walls. After this surgery Dwosiya become a full-time employee in a prestigious underground bordello in Machnattan-the central borough of Old Kroy City. Working hard, with an overtimes, she become soon a leading performer in the sex acts. In three months of employment she become

11

very famous and was included in Guinness Book of World Records for extracting 18(!) pounds of urine from a client- a 58-year old judge- when he collapsed into an orgasm during an oral sex.

This unexpected strike of luck soon attracted attention of several Pollypood producers and she was invited for a numerous auditions including the slumber sessions. After sleeping with 5 producers at the same mating spell of time and performing precisely calculated (after the consultations with ingenious inventor Haim) body movements during the intercourse sessions with 5 producers, her vagina become five angle-star shaped. After this vagina modifications, she become a Pollypood star and had roles in 5 light budgeted movies. Two movies were completely shot in a men's toilet and three movies-in a women's toilet. She also had dated a young highly decorated actor whom she met on a party throwing by the actor celebrating a milestone in his penis adventure- a victorious exit from a vagina #5000. At the same night Dwosiya became his woman #5001. After passionate month long romance and after Dwosiya had successfully transmitted to him a gonorrhea from one of the producers, they decided to get married.

While receiving a treatment for gonorrhea, the fiancé had requested that Dwosiya introduced him to the person from whom she got this sexually transmitted disease to thank him for adding such a joyful excitement to his life. Dwosiya was not sure who gave her the disease so she introduced him to all five producers. All seven become so friendly that the start performing a "mini-orgy" parties, namely the sex sessions involving Dwosiya and six partners. These parties were so sweet that they decided to prepare for a wedding present a special project under code name "Magnificent Seven". The goal was to achieve simultaneous orgasms in all seven members (while six males were accommodated by Dwosiya's vagina, anal opening, mouth and the fists) just before saying the famous "I do!" After 24 rehearsal sessions they finally succeeded but the project was abandoned after Dwosiya, while on her way in a taxi cab to pick-up the wedding dress, fell in love for 17 minutes with another passenger in taxi- a young handsome hulk. They had a passionate sex on a back seat of the taxi cab and Dwosiya got in a couple days a nasty and persistent yeast infection that caused blood in her urine and an unbearable burning inside the penises of her six partners just in time for the wedding ceremony.

After the wedding the newly married couple had moved to an expensive ranch with a beautiful house on the property. The most salient feature of the house was an existence of 15 unisex toilets. In toilets #1 thru #5 the toilet's user was practicing yoga with the help of an yoga instructor specializing in only one certain yoga posture. After finishing all five postures with a help of 5 male and 5 female yoga instructors, the toilet's user was mentally prepared for the process of waste extraction. In toilets #6 thru #10 the physical bowel movement result in successful advance of the waste half way to the exit from the body (again, with the help of 5 male and 5 female massagers). In toilets #11 thru #15 the waste was pushed further, and finally in toilet #15 the waste was leaving the body and by free fall reached it's final destination- the golden surface of toilet water. In toilets #11 thru #15 a special machinery for spraying an aromatic aerosol into the air was employed to kill the unwanted smell. After the process of waste extraction was completed, the male/female cleaner in toilet #15 have cleaned and washed the rectum area of the user. The waste extraction adventure become a real joyful and painless experience and, when the toilet workers went on strike together with the other members of an union- The International Brotherhood of Toilet Engineers- Local T12, Local T22, Dwosiya and her husband were suffering for 2 weeks from the constipation and the diarrhea.

But the fresh country air made some unexpected changes in the husband's brain chemistry. After 5 months of life together, Dwosiya's husband become an animal lover, raped all animals in his ranch and in the neighboring ranches and later initiated a bitter divorce battle with Dwosiya in order to become a free man and marry a cow with a green pensive eyes from his friend's ranch.

But nothing could stop Dwosiya on her way to become a world champion for a second time. With Haim's help she was undertaken another plastic surgery. At this time during the surgery four round reinforcing quarter inch in diameter thick bars made of steel were inserted inside of each of Dwosiya's breasts and a liner made of stainless steel was inserted along her vagina's walls. These crenellation measures allowed Dwosiya to be able to have an intercourse with 1200 males in 24 hour period without interruption which represents another world record and another paragraph in Guinness Book of World Records. The whole intercourse session can be viewed at www.queensizevagina.edu.

1.  THE DIAMOND
The diamond our gang of four bought from a swindler in exchange for almost all of their belongings turned out to be of a poor quality. As an excuse ingenious inventor Haim had proclaimed that this happened because of some kind of chemical reaction between the diamond and the waste holding liquid he swallowed during the smuggling operation in the custom hall in the City of Brest. The money received for selling the diamond to another swindler- an owner of a jewelry store on Prighton Peach Avenue- were enough only to bribe a super of an apartment building to allow our symbols to rent an apartment in said building which was under Section 8 (also known as a Program 8) where the rent is divided between the city and the tenant, the City paying to the landlord almost all the rent's money.

(To be continued.)

Learn about Surka's wrestling career, her cheating on Haim; learn about further modification of Dwosia's vagina- compartmentation, inside threading e.t.c.)

## QUIZ # 1

1. What is the best description of the stuff above?

       a.  Garbage!
       b.  Good!
       c.  Disgusting!
       d.  Classic humor!
       e.  Disgusting but close to the truth.

14

2. How many pounds of the hard digestive food is available for the gas production by Surka?

       a.  1 pound;
       b.  5 pounds;
       c.  50 pounds;
       d.  20 pounds.

# ADVENTURE
## IN
## LAW

### "THERE IS NO LAW-
### LAWYERS ARE!"

The Stinking justice system in the Divided Regions of Antarctica must be completely overhauled.

How often, in the Divided Regions of Antarctica, you can hear on TV, in the movies and in the real life the following sentence:

### "You need a good lawyer!"

You think deeper and realize the sinister essence of this sentence-

### "A good lawyer!", not "a good law!"

This means that the equal justice proclaimed in the Constitution of the Divided Regions of Antarctica is simple a joke or (if you come closer so I can whisper in your ear), it's a **LIE**.

The existing institution of private lawyers is **UNCONSTITUTION- AL CRIMINAL ENTERPRISE** (since it violates the Constitution requirements for the equal justice) and creates a fruitful ground for the crime flourishing. The most dangerous lawyers are the good lawyers which become rich and famous once they complete the brilliant work for letting free the murderers, rapists, e.t.c. Good lawyers/judges have established a network of a domestic terror which is more dangerous than the terrorists outside of the Divided Regions of Antarctica.

If your money can get you a good lawyer you can easily get away with the murder as we have witnessed in the real life.

Thanks to a good lawyers, the innocent people are in prison and the murderers walking free on our streets. In the meantime the good lawyers become a movie and TV stars enjoying the good life spending the money covered with the blood of the victims.

Our justice system stinks so badly that it is time to dismantle it. We can smell the stench of the system right from TV screens. The antiquated system came from the middle ages and the only significant positive improvement is that the lawyers/judges not wearing the wigs eliminating the scary scarecrow appearance. All the other improvements upon the system were made to maximize the profit for the lawyers/judges.

Now just listen to a true typical story.

There was a terrible auto accident and the victim suppose to get several millions of insurance money (the insurance company agreed to pay). Of course the lawyers also must receive millions in the insurance money (for what? The lawyers were no harmed in an accident and are in very good health. Millions for shifting the paper! Good job, isn't it? That's why every second youngster in the Divided Regions of Antarctica want to be a lawyer!). The judge that had handled the case , become very angry that the lawyers will get big bucks and he will have only the salary so he start dragging the case and requested the bribe from the lawyer representing the plaintiff. But the lawyer was a good one and he got wired himself and caught the judge requesting the bribe on a tape.

When the judge was confronted with a bribe allegation the first thing he did was a compete denial.(The judge happen to be a liar! What can you expect from a liar?) But then the good lawyer representing the judge have persuaded the judge to plead guilty so that another fellow judge can give him the minimum sentence (from a fork 3 to 9 years he will get only 3 years in prison while the regular criminal-not a judge-can get 9 years). After special treatment in prison (again the treatment of a judge in prison is much better than that of a regular criminal, it's like a little vacation!) he can have a honorable retirement with a full pension. That's how the judges rape the system! By the way, the fork offers another opportunity for the judges to show a real power. If the judge the night before sentencing a convicted criminal had a constipation or a diarrhea and came in the morning in a bad mood, the convict will get the maximum but if the judge had during the night a successful sex with a spouse and came in the morning in a good mood the convict will get a minimum. This way the judge is a min-god. He decided, not the law!

Everybody on the planet Earth recalls the trial of a rich businessman who killed his ex-wife and her two friends (which was confirmed by DNA tests) and the "mean team" of lawyers together with 12 jurors determine that the murders were performed by the UFO crew prompting the Fine Bureau of Information and the Interpol to set the ambushes at all known UFO landing sites in order to catch the real killer(s)!

We repeat: in years good lawyers/judges created a criminal network of a domestic terror. The striking difference between the terrorists and a good lawyers is that the terrorists can be punished and a good lawyers become rich and famous for successfully raping the law!

My fellow antarctidians!

The lawyers/judges will never change the system since it is a very profitable business but we, **THE PEOPLE**, can! After all, how many lawyers we have in the Divided Regions of Antarctica? 300,000? 500,000? But we, the people,we are in millions! We shall prevail!

Is there a solution? Yes, it is!

Science and technology!

The first stage of a process-COLLECTION OF EVIDENCE- must be upgraded utilizing the modern technology. Nobody can believe that with up-to-date technology (even space technology!) we can not find who did it! Right here is the place for a lawyer (we call him a law enforcer!)- with a detective team- to make sure that the evidence is collected in accordance with the law!

The second stage of a process-THE TRIAL-shall be scientified and computerized!

Let's get our geeks and nerds to work! In no time all the laws will be programmed and several CD-roms will replace the tons of books that the lawyers must study. THE COMPUTER is the best lawyer, the best judge and the best juror!

The trial become a simple process of inserting the evidence data into the computer programmed in accordance with the law. The judge will conduct the process of inserting the evidence into the computer and 12 jurors will witness the process with all their comments and objections resolved at the spot by the computer. The output of the computer is the VERDICT! Simple, inexpensive, scientifically correct and, most of all, fairreal equal justice! Since there is one program for all instances up to the "main frame" constantly upgraded by the Supreme Court judges no more shifting the verdict from one circuit to another, no more "sustained", "overruled", "plea bargaining", "inadmissible", "your honor", "beyond reasonable doubts", "double jeopardy", "perjury", "jury tampering" and all other lawyers bull created to produce a "DRECK" at the end of the trial (refer to German-English dictionary for a "DRECK" definition). No more law practicing by the lawyers, e.g. no more raping the law!

We repeat: lawyers/judges will never change the system because of the high profit for the lawyers and the judges at the expense of the human lives.

We have to change the **stinking** system.

That is why we urge you to join our **PAL (People Against Lawyers)** organization. Our goals:

1. Computerize the system! Create programs for all law clauses, insert them into the computer network with a "main frame" controlled and modified by the Supreme Court judges.
2. Replace the trial by the jurors with a trial by the computer! Trial by the jurors stinks! With the same evidence different jury will return different verdict. Hang jury is a brilliant proof that **jurors can not do their job!** The goddess of justice must be blindfolded. But the jurors have their eyes wide open. They evaluate the lawyer's performance, the sex, the age, the look, the race and not the evidence as a crucial factor in returning the verdict. As it proved right now, by the DNA testing, the jury together with the good lawyers put innocent people in prison and let the murders go free!
3. Upgrade the collection of evidence into scientific process utilizing the highest achievements of science and technology for the money saved when the lawyers will not be paid for frivolous cases.
4. Instead of teaching our children how to kill and dismember the human body we can teach them the law. By the high school graduation time they will know the law better then contemporary

lawyer. The law is simple: don't kill!, don't steal!, don't rape!, don't embezzle! and so on...

What a beauty will be this new system! The law software will be available for everybody. There will be no trial unless the computer shows the conviction! Computer is not interested in the wealth, race, age, gender of the accused –EQUAL JUSTICE!

Our first appeal for a membership in our organization is to relatives of the killed victims who's murderers are walking free, thanks to a good lawyers!

Finally the word for the lawyers:

We are not against the big bucks they making. Let pay them even more but for the **enforcing the law** –not **practicing the law!** Word "lawyer" must disappear leaving the first half of it-the"LAW!"

### QUIZ # 2

1. On a scale of 0% to 100% what is in your opinion the percentage of corrupt judges in the existing justice system in the Divided Regions of Antarctica?
    - A. Less than 10%;
    - B. 10%-30%;
    - C. 30%-50%;
    - D. 50%-75%;
    - E. More than 75%.

2. If a good lawyer performed so well that the jury acquitted the murderer, should the good lawyer be considered as an accessory to the murder?
    - A. Yes!
    - B. No!

3. Does the existing justice system in the Divided Regions of Antarctica stink?
    - A. Yes!
    - B. No!

4. Does the trial by the jury stink?
    - A. Yes!
    - B. No!

5. Will you join the **PAL(People Against Lawyers)** organization?
    - A. Yes!
    - B. No!

# ADVENTURE
# IN
# POLITICS

An accidental people illiterate in politics run the fictitious country- the Divided Regions of Antarctica.

olitical life in the Divided Regions of Antarctica is also full of laughter.
After the tragic events, the government officially promised to find the people responsible for the disaster. Even a special commission was formed (the lawyers need a couple of millions of taxpayers money to make the ends meet!). We think that in government's statement we have the existence of a little humor, thus forcing us to help the government with a couple of hints as follows:

1.  What about the high ranking guys/gals in the airport security? It seems like everybody (thanks to TV and the newspapers) but they knew that the security stinks. Shouldn't these fellows be at least free on bail charged with the criminal negligence?
2.  What about the lawyers-politicians that cut that money for the right operation of Cute Information Authority giving them only the amount enough to spy on their own spouses. Even now, with the money they have, they can only get the information as follows:

"We expecting something! This could be a nuclear hit or a biological hit or some kind of explosions somewhere, sometimes. But don't worry! Just stay closer to your beloved cemetery and, in case the hit will materialize, without panic crawl to your designated grave and die in orderly fashion!"

At the same time a huge amount of money was allocated for the Fine Bureau of Information to resolve the issues connected with the following great tasks:

1.  From what part of Nancy Cougar's body was former Secondary State Treasurer Michael Brandon's penis withdrawn just before the sperm extraction on the Nancy's dress? Was it from:
    a.  The first?
    b.  The mouth?
    c.  The rectum?
    d.  The vagina?
    e.  The other space(specify:)?
2.  Was Nancy also in the state of orgasm during the sperm extraction?
3.  If the sperm extraction was a result of the masturbation, how many hands were involved?

4. Was the former Secondary State Treasurer Michael Brandon's penis directed just to the Bronek River or to a specific National Monument?
5. What was the exact amount of the sperm left in former Secondary State Treasurer M. Brandon's testicles? Was it in the amount enough to run the country?

We hope that these two hints will help the government in their endeavors.

To rephrase the famous sentence ("The Butler did it!")we with a full confidence can conclude our small research by proclaiming:

"The **penis** did it!"

The penis of the former Secondary State Treasurer Michael Brandon, that is!

Subsequently, the said penis become an Historic entity; the replica of the penis was manufactured in actual size (in erected state, of course!),the actual shape, color and texture and was positioned for public view in world famous Madame Tussaud's wax museum.

After several days almost 75% of the penis was destroyed by the zealous females trying to repeat the historic oral sex sessions performed by Nancy Cougar on an original former Secondary State Treasurer Michael Brandon's penis. While in the state of an orgasm, the horny females were piercing their teeth with a tremendous force into the flesh of the wax duplicate of the penis, chipping away the parts of the penis.

Even the steel hedge around the penis with a barbed wire connected to a high voltage couldn't stop the above referenced females. Six of them were eventually electrocuted and two of them are now in a hospital in a critical (but stable!) condition.

The wax museum administration decided to sell the remaining 25% of the wax duplicate on B-Bay. In 24 hours all the remnants were sold with a huge profit; the money received were spend the same day- famous artist made a colorful picture of the penis in a state of sperm extraction. The picture is now on a display protected by the enclosure made of a bulletproof glass.

By the way, we even now don't have all the answers to all the questions referenced above. Only part of the answers to the tasks were released to the public, although we eligible for reviewing all the answers by the Freedom of Information Act.

Even at present we can see the former Secondary State Treasurer on TV, but he is so shy, that he is telling nothing about the lovely time his penis had with the mouth of naïve gal. Instead he is talking some boring staff that doesn't excite anyone. The same thing with his friend, bureverend Pussy Pullman, which is also so shy and telling nothing about hard work he had performed in the wrong vagina and manufactured a child by mistake!

Since we have already touched the romantic relationship between the former Secondary State Treasurer Michael Brandon's penis and Nancy

Cougar's mouth (this part of answers was revealed! It was an oral sex!) we must now in logical sequence recall the "procratch-do not procratch" game created by the lawyers.

Those were the Days!

The stock market and the whole country completely were on the brink of collapse. The unions threatened with the general strike! Some bureverends predicted not only powerful earthquakes but a real end of the world if the procratchment will go through!

But, thank goodness, by the very precise measurements, it was established that the weight of the sperm on Nancy Cougar's dress was about 13.74% short for the procratchment. This fact plus the fact (as the Fine Bureau of Information confirmed) that Nancy was singing the national anthem while holding the former Secondary State Treasurer Michael Brandon's penis in her mouth plus another fact (also confirmed by the Fine Bureau of Information) that the former Secondary State Treasurer, while extracting the sperm, was crying and whispering the names of the two people he was really in love with-his wife Lolita and his daughter (I forgot her name!) persuaded the government people not to procratch. To proof the singing experience by Nancy, a multimillion equipment (bought ,of course, for taxpayer's money) was used to produce computerized analysis of the distribution of residual traces of DNA from Nancy's saliva along the erected penis of the former Secondary State Treasurer Michael Brandon and comparison with the acoustical spectrum of the first and the last words of the national anthem. The unexpected difficulties to erect the penis for testing were easily overcome when a nude photograph of a former gal (with whom the former Secondary State Treasure was cheating on his wife before Nancy and who was suing former Secondary State Treasurer for the incorrect sex ) plus another woman who recently made the allegations that the former Secondary State Treasurer Michael Brandon raped her-both in a promiscuous positions- were presented before former Secondary State Treasurer's eyes after unsuccessful attempts to erect the penis by showing the nude photo of his wife in the similar position. While collecting the DNA samples along the former Secondary State Treasurer's penis, the testing lab also found DNA traces on a main body in the vicinity of the base of the penis which with 99% accuracy proved that the penis was completely inside the Nancy's mouths and the traces of the DNA on the main body were coming even from Nancy's lips. In other words, the oral sex was a 100% perfect job and several porn movie producers proposed a lucrative contracts to Nancy to become a porn star specializing mainly on the oral sex performances but Nancy had refused these business propositions. In addition, the lawyers were already, like the spider with the fly's blood, saturated with the money swindled during the whole process.

The whole sequence of the sperm extraction is described in the new book by former Secondary State Treasurer Michael Brandon in Chapter 4:

**"Blow job and it's role in making monetary and foreign policy decisions".**

But the real positive outcome of the "procratch-do not procratch" game was the election of the scorned wife Lolita to the Secondary Tier. The people of Old Kroy State felt that she is in the possession of the two features required for the representation of their interests in the Administration, namely:

1. She is a lawyer;
2. She is a liar (she lied together with the husband in the first phase-phase of denial of any relationship between the penis of the former Secondary State Treasurer and the mouth of the naïve gal Nancy).

These features plus the stainless throat were the items that brought her the victory in the Elections.

By more deeper analysis, the whole idea of "procratch-do- not pro-cratch" game was wrong from the beginning and was dragged only because thousands can make a good living utilizing the lust in the kinky sex between playboy-Secondary State Treasurer and a very naïve gal. The History provided us with the examples of a Great Political Figures being passionate playboys and playgirls.

Consider for example The Greatest Playgirl of all times-Russian Tsaritsa Emmanuela the Twenty-Eights the Great who ordered tight pants to be wearing by the Russian Army officers so that the size of the penis was clearly identified. With all the Great penises she made an intercourse. But the appetite of her vagina for a tremendous size of penises led her to a fatal end. Not satisfied with the sizes of the penises by the human beings she decided to have sex with a stallion with an enormous organ. Special facilities were built and a special equipment was utilized for the intercourse. For almost half an hour the stallion work very hard and after unloading the sperm inside Tsaritsa's vagina he started the process of withdrawing the apparatus from the vagina. At this time one of the noble men ("boyarin") who had witnessed the process together with a bunch of others hit the stallion in order to speed up the withdrawal. The stallion startled and made a powerful jerk. Together with the penis a big portion of Tsaritsa's guts were accidentally withdrawn. Since there were not our times and there were no such great surgeons as we have now (remember the surgery when the penis cut off by enraged jealous wife was sewed back in place and the husband even become a porn star with the penis operating even better than before), the Tsaritsa soon died. While Tsaritsa was enjoying the Great sex life, Russia have waged victorious wars because the Russian soldiers were inspired by the above mentioned vagina's passion for the Great penises.

Or take another example also from the history of Russia- the adventures of Pafnutiy Pachnutiew –former monk with a 13 inch long penis(when hard, of course!).

The penis took an unforgettable journeys thru the vaginas of Russian aristocrat's wives. It is still questionable whether it was inside the Tsaritsa's vagina. Most historians think it was not and the only the influence on Tsaritsa was achieved through the healing power of Pafnutiy who he used to heal the Tsaritsa's very ill son. In addition, Pafnutiy also was a good hypnotist. Thanks to an enormous size of Pafnutiy's penis he achieved position equal to the Tsar's and was assassinated by the jealous aristocrats-the husbands of the wives with spoiled vaginas. The assassination of Pafnutiy led to an October Revolution and a siege of the power in Russia by the Bolsheviks (Communists).

Or consider now the adventures of another playboy-a preformer Secondary State Treasurer of the Divided Regions of Antarctica- James Filip Kramer, who shared a very famous Pollypood actress with his brother and another fellows. The rumor is that he had even a "ménage the trios" during the working hours. After his assassination, his wife who loved him very much had married an nemetian billionaire Bypussys. After she died, the children decided to punish their father and had buried their mother not next to the latest husband but next to James Filip Kramer, so that poor James Filip Kramer now had to inhale the Bypussys's DNA up to the end of his life up there (in the other world, that is).

So, as you can see now, the greatest playboys and playgirls were real historical figures.

Or consider now the playboys inside the clergy! Let us start with an unforgettable Bureverend Pussy Pullman, who once wanted to be a Prime Administrator in the Divided States of Antarctica and then suddenly dropped out of the race in fear that the meticulous journalists soon find out that he had manufactured a child working hard in a wrong vagina-not inside his wife's vagina. Ironically it was at the same time when the Bureverend was lamenting together with the penis of the former Secondary State Treasurer Brandon while the former Secondary State Treasurer himself was under the procratchment scare and had to navigate his wife's vagina which was a very boring process and could not be compared to navigation inside the mouth of the naïve gal Nancy Cougar full of delicious saliva's moisture and warmth that was spread around his penis by Nancy's vibrating tongue.

Or an army of the priests who had screwed up the rectums and the vaginas of the underage boys and girls.

Some of these priests were put to trial and even convicted. They, probably, didn't have a good lawyers who right away could successfully defend them by attracting the attention of the jurors to the three very important items.

Item #1. Due to the global warming of our planet the temperature and the pressure of the sperm inside the priest's testicles could reach a critical point and the mass of the violent sperm must be unloaded, or it can hit the brain causing non-repairable damage to the brain or the testicles themselves could be blown out. The good lawyer can always find a good doctor who will testify that if the sperm will hit the brain, the priest will pronounce in all English words letter "B" instead of letter "A" causing unprecedented difficulties for the flock to understand the priest and this is practically eliminate priest's ability to do the fine work.

In addition, to resolve the problem a good lawyer can suggest that the sensors for the measurements of the temperature and the pressure of the sperm can be mounted on the priest's testicles and when these variables will reach the critical point the signal light positioned on the priest's pants will operate to show that the priest is ready for mating and the young girls/boys can **voluntarily** have sex with the priest.

<u>Item #2.</u> The prolonged sexual abstinence is a leading factor in the development of a prostate cancer. Do we want to harm our beloved priests this way? Of course, not!

<u>Item #3.</u> The priests simply have found another channel of communication and instead of the ears have used the rectums and the vaginas utilizing the sperm from their testicles as a lubricant to minimize the mechanical friction and the electrical resistance to the words coming from the priest's mouth.

In addition we're positive that there exists somewhere in the Divided Regions of Antarctica a religious sect created by another unsuccessful opera singer or a janitor and this sect is practicing the rape of the youngsters as a part of a natural process. Why not letting our priests to be converted into their believes instead of putting them in prison?

In the year 5002 there will be a Prime Administrator Elections in the Divided Regions of Antarctica but we can start evaluating the chances of the possible candidates right now.

A.  For Attorney General!
Any murderer or rapist acquitted by the jury as a result of a brilliant work by a good lawyer.
His jingle:
   "The System Deserves It's General!"

B.  For the head of Drug Elimination Authority!
The former Prime Capital City Official who was destroying the drugs in a very forceful manner-by using them!
      Just Imagine!

The Prime City Official (and we are talking about the Capital of the Divided Regions of Antarctica! Shame on you, Antarctica!) is using the drugs, get caught on a tape shown doing drugs in an hotel and brought to a trial! But remember: there is no Law, the Lawyers are in the Divided Regions of Antarctica! The guy has good money to hire a good lawyers and he did! The good lawyers for good money quickly persuaded the jurors that the Prime City Official came to the hotel for an oral sex sessions and not for doing drugs. This way it was possible to arrange for a Prime City Official a short vacation in a federal prison (one of the tabloids even informed us that he had a real oral sex session while in prison, serving the light sentence. At the same time, the other inmates could only afford the services of a fat, spayed prison's female cat which was licking the inmate's penises covered with sour cream saved by the inmates after several lunches and smuggled inside the prison cells). The low class guy for the same crime could get behind the bars for a long, long time.

After the Prime City Official got a little bit of a rehabilitation (less than a year!) he become again a Prime City Official!

What a country! What a lawyers! What a stench of the system! What a LAUGH!

C. For a Prime Administrator!

C.a. Former Secondary State Treasurer Michael Brandon!

We have already prepared for him an Election Jingle. It goes like this:

" I run for a Prime Administrator position for two reasons:

The reason #1: To fight the poverty by building more traffic lights!

The reason #2: To correct misspelled word as follows:

In the sentence "WHITE BUILDING" in word "WHITE" replace the letters "IT" with the letters "OR".

C.b. The scorned wife of the former Secondary State Treasurer Michael Brandon- Lolita Brandon together with Nancy Cougar. Their Jingles:

#1 "Lolita for Nancy's Diet- Salad with Sec's sperm Dress-ing.

#2. "Lolita For Prime, Nancy For Vice!"

Coming to the Secondary Tier on a Great Tide created by perfect oral sex performance by Nancy Cougar on her husband's male organ of generation, Lolita Brandon has the most real chances to get the Prime Administrator position together with the said Nancy as a team mate (as a vice!).

Also, don't forget Lolita's two most valuable features: 1. She is a lawyer and 2. She is a liar (she lied together with her husband in the first phase –the phase of denial by the former Secondary State Treasurer Michael Brandon the affair with Nancy Cougar). These two features are the most precious features of the most of today's politicians in Divided Regions of Antarctica.

As we can see, the political circle is full of accidental people. It become a good manner to push the criminals to the top. Right now several former jailbirds are preparing themselves to run for a Prime Administrator position! And they will!

The rumor is that the lawyers pushing right now for a legislature to accept the law requiring that before the person can run for a Prime Administrator position, he/she must be jailed for at least three times. And this is very logical. The guys/gals will have the best experience in the crime business and will do their best to make sure that the criminal enterprise will flourish, so that the lawyers can multiply their profit. But this is from another adventure! At this time I urge you-the readers- to join our organization – **PAL (People Against Lawyers)** to call for a clean-up of the political stable.

Dear Antarctidians!

Who are our politicians?

The lawyers, the sportsmen, the movie stars (including the porn stars which again underlines our concepts about the importance of the genitals behavior), clergy guys (wait a minute! what clergy has to do with a politics? This is **unconstitutional!** Lawyers! Where are you? By the Constitution of the Divided Regions of Antarctica the clergy position must be separated from the State position. Either the lawyers are so illiterate that hey didn't read the Constitution or they are waiting for anther couple millions of taxpayers money in order to straighten this out!),the businessmen, e.t.c. Most of them are completely illiterate in politics.

**The country must be run by the scientists-
not by the accidental people illiterate in politics!**

Our universities must teach students to become a politician and must have courses in political science, computers, economics, mathematics and other related subjects and not the science how to screw up the law! And the best graduate must become a Prime Administrator!

### QUIZ # 3

1. Based on the experience of the penis of the former Secondary State Treasurer Michael Brandon, should the autobiography of the penis be submitted for a public review by every candidate for the Prime Administrator position (or another high political position ) and should this autobiography be considered a major issue?
   A. Yes!
   B. No!

2. Recently, on the antarctidian radio, a woman described in details how she was raped by the former Secondary State Treasurer Michael Brandon. At that time she didn't press charges, and Lolita Brandon-the wife of the Secondary State Treasurer-had thanked her. Would you believe the woman?
   A. Yes!
   B. No!
   C. No opinion!

HINT: Think twice before answering the question above because if you select answer 'A', you inadvertently imply that the Treasure Department in a State Government was run by a rapist e. g. a criminal. Consider better answer 'C'!

3. The same woman, further, suggested that Lolita Brandon in her book (for which she got a good chunk of money-several millions!) incorrectly had informed the readers about the time she had realized that the husband had an oral sex sessions with Nancy Cougar. The woman alleged that the Lolita knew about the affair long before the date mentioned in the book. Based on this, on the scale from 0% to 100%, what is the percentage of the truth in the Lolita's book?
    A.  0%-no truth at all!
    B.  0%-15%;
    C.  15%-50%;
    D.  50%-75%.
    E.  100%- All truth!

4. Should the priest with a violent penis be considered a pioneer discovering new communication channels or a criminal?
    A.  A pioneer!
    B.  A criminal!

5. In your opinion, on a scale from 0% to 100%, what is the percentage of the priests with the penises penetrating the vaginas and the rectums of the youngsters?
    A.  Less than 25%;
    B.  25%-50%;
    C.  50%-75%;
    D.  More than 75%.

# ADVENTURE
# IN
# ADVERTISEMENT

Spruce up the advertisement!

After filtrating thru the ears for the twelfth(!) time the ubiquitous sen- tence "What are you waiting for?" we feel there is an undeveloped region of the possibilities in the advertising. Take for example an utilization of the rhymes, although it seems that the English is not inclined to the rhymes in the degree comparable with Spanish or Italian.

Let's start with the first commercial developed for this magazine.

> **ENOUGH TOUGH STUFF!**
> **READ "THE LAUGH" !**                                   (#1)

The second example reflects the deep feelings every antarctidian wants to express regarding one of the most important government's deed:

> **FIGHT AIDS –**
> **USE CONDOM!**
> **FIGHT TAXES –**
> **USE NO CONDOM!**                                       (#2)

or more romantic version:

> **SEX HEALS,**
> **TAX KILLS!**                                           (#3)

After another murderer acquitted by the jury as a result of a brilliant work by a good lawyer the following jingle is in order:

> **FIGHT CRIME –**
> **KILL LAWYERS!**                                        (#4)

Of course, the word "kill" is used in indirect sense!

Further exploration of the previous slogan leads us to a bit controversial idea:

> **FIGHT DRUGS –**
> **KILL USERS!**                                          (#5)

The idea is controversial because we can not live without the elite of our society-the top portion that has big bucks. Almost every day we hear a victorious statements from the police: eliminated another drug ring and destroyed drugs in the amount worth so many millions and so many millions and so on. Who uses these drugs? A junkies on the street? We doubt it! The drugs are used by the elite of our society! So why hunt and jail the drug dealers? They simply doing the business! If we can not live without the elite, we have to legalize the drugs the same way we legalize the booze! After all, people have the right to kill themselves-this is the ultimate luxury they can afford. They have already everything-money, expensive cars and houses, sex with the thousands of partners, so the life become not exited anymore!

Let's now try to advertise our big and powerful corporations. They moved our lifestyle to the unbelievable level of progress. The name of the corporations are misspelled since we have no permission to advertise the real corporations. Also there are some misspelled words so you can have an active participation in our discussion.

First, a little bit boring jingle with the rhyme:

**Giant in Motion-**
**I am**
**J M !** (#6)

Simple! But is it striking enough to emphasize the power of a real legendary corporation?

Another example for the communication giants:

**CALLING HORIZON**
**EXPAND WITH**
**HERIZON!** (#7)

And

**Y**
    **T**
        **and**
           **T!**
**The best**
    **EN**
      **TI**
        **TY!** (#8)

Concise:

**NO – CRACK!**
**YES – NAC!** (#9)

Combined with:

**NO – SMOKE!**
**YES – MOKE!** (#10)

For the competition we can suggest:

**NEXT THING?**
**BERGER KING!** (#11)

Another example of a further development for #10;

**AFTER PLAYING**
**CHESS or POLO**
**QUENCH YOUR THIRST**
**WITH**
**SUKA COLA!** (#12)

For several days we try to invent something for the competition and suddenly the dynamic slogan consisting of two consecutive screens:

**Please**
(This is a first screen)

**Imagine**
**Plush**
**Sip!**
**It is**                                                    (#13)

In the second screen only the first letters on each line remain producing the name of the corporation by reading vertically:

P
I
P
S
I                                                          (#14)

Exploring double meaning and a rhyme:

**LIFE IS DULL?**
**VISIT TAJ MAHAL!**                                        (#15)

What Taj Mahal? Is it tourist agency from India who advertise this or
is it something else? Just imaging the combination of #15 with flashing
sequentially hearts, diamonds, clubs and spades on a uniform wearing by
the employees of (you know who's)!

Let's go shopping!

**ENJOY SHOPPING ART**
**IN BULLMART!**                                            (#16)

One of the biggest corporations deserves a variation. For example:

**USE BULLMART**
**FOR**
**SHOPPING SMART!**                                         (#17)

Let's take a vacation:

**TIRED?**
**SAD?**
**TRY**
**CLUB NED!**                                               (#18)

I would like to see #18 also on a uniform for "crazy people" who are
giving us unforgettable fantastic vacation time.

The idea of a globalization in advertisement realized in a following
"global advertisement layout":

**D R A = WE +**                                            (#19)


**. . . . . . . . . .**
                                                            (#20)

where on line (#20) can be positioned in sequence the companies
who are really part of our lives and a part of what we call a DIVIDED
REGIONS of ANTARCTICA

The first corporation on line (#20) in unison with our love for rhymes
we suggest:

**S B S !**

And stabilizing it by adding:

    **NO STRESS**

    **WITH  S B S !**             (#21)

More rhymes for more corporations:

    **ON COMPUTER PLANET'S**

    **LOFT-**

    **PROUD GIANT-**

    **NICROMOFT!**             (#22)

or

    **CYBRO "SWELL"**

    **COMPU "BELL"**             (#23)

or a "soap opera's" style:

    **USING THIS**

    **SHINING TEETH**

    **CALL IT GREAT**

    **"TOLGATE"**             (#24)

and so on.

It is also our intent to introduce a concept of a "negative advertisement", which, in our opinion, is more productive than the traditional positive advertisement. To begin the experimenting with this concept, we urge the readers to describe on the next page with a heading

LEMON'S GROVE

all defective items they bought together with the manufacturer's name, telephone # (if available) and model number. We will then confront the manufacturer and hopefully the matter will be resolved to the satisfaction of all parties involved.

# LEMON'S GROVE

Many organizations have expressed an interest in sponsoring this interactive book.
We selected several of them…

#1
"Y & Z CHAMELEONS"-ATTORNEYS AT LAW:
a)

**"Y & Z CHAMELEONS"!**
**We thrive on your crimes!**

b)

"As our name suggests, we,"Y & Z Chameleons", are utilizing our tongues (the same way as the famous lizards) to make a living, and we change our color from red (offensive, prosecution) to green (defensive, counselor) depending on the party paying us more money.

Thanks to the laws, we-the lawyers- wrote, we have already murderers and rapists as young as 10 years old, so with a confidence we are looking into our future which will be more profitable then ever before!"

And c)

"We-"Y & Z Chameleons", Attorneys at law, are very proud to present our new "FREQUENT KILLER PROGRAM" for people who have enough money to pay our fees.

The program works as follows:

If you kill in pairs (or, even better, in triplets), we guarantee that we will brainwash the jurors by utilizing the double jeopardy clause, so you always will be acquitted on all murder related charges.

For each killing you receive a certain amount of points. For example:

Murder in first degree- 100 points;
Murder in second degree-75 points;
Manslaughter-50 points and so on!

After you collected 1125 points, our services for next double killing are free, which means a big savings to you!

We also have low discount rates for parolees!"

#2
NorthSouthEastWest Bank
**"You pay off your loan and we will
Give you another one to buy briefs
For yourself and panties for her!"**

#3
U F O Crew
**"We'll screw up your brains and we'll
Chew up your genitals in 21 st century!
U F O !
Our heads are made of Bermuda Triangles!"**

## QUIZ #4

1. Is it a good idea to create a "jingle wholesale" company for the advertisement utilizing more rhymes and dynamic structures consisting
   from several screens?
       A. Yes!
       B. No!

2. Is it a good idea to perform a "NEGATIVE ADVERTISEMENT"?
       A. Yes!
       B. No!

3. What slogan is a good one?
       A. None.
       B. #.........

# APOLOGY

Once again, we urge the readers not to compare the life in the Divided Regions of Antarctica with the life in the United States of America, where we have the best lawyers and the best judges in the whole world, a real heroes! In USA we also have the sharpest and the smartest politicians, the bright raw models for new generations.

We apologize for any inconvenience we inadvertently created for this people.

We created a fictitious country-a Divided Regions of Antarctica-in order to get a "stuff ready for laugh" just to talk, to interact and to laugh!

## FINAL QUIZ

1. Does it make sense to write next interactive book (#2)?
   A. Yes!
   B. No!

2. Would you like to buy the next book?
   A. Yes!
   B. No!

3. If you want to buy the next book, what is the maximum dollar amount you are ready to spend on it?
   A. Under $5.
   B. $5-$10.
   C. &11-$15.
   D. &16-$20.
   E. More than $20 (specify exact amount).

If the answers to the questions 1 & 2 we'll get from you are "B"s, or if you not answering at all, we want to thank you for reading this book and say " Good-bye!" If you want to reply, send all answers to all the quizzes, send your corrections to the misspelled words, or if you want to say any-thing at all, please communicate thru the following e:mail addresses shown on the next page:

| If you reside in: | E:mail address: | Reply on the following dates of each month: |
| --- | --- | --- |
| NorthEast | A2atol@aol.com | 1-15 |
| SouthEast | B3rina@aol.com | 16-31 |
| NorthWest | N12ly@aol.com | 1-15 |
| SouthWest | B9jak@aol.com | 16-31 |
| All other States | S7epav@aol.com | 1-15 |

46